minno®

LAUGH AND GROW® BIBLE FOR KIDS

FAMILY EASTER DEVOTIONAL

Written by **Jess Wolstenholm, M. Ed.**
and **Christie Thomas**

This book belongs to ______________________________

Given by ______________________________

On ______________________________

Minno Press
818 18th Ave S
10th Floor
Nashville, TN 37203

laughandgrowbible.com | gominno.com/press

Written by Jess Wolstenholm, M. Ed.
and Christie Thomas

Editorial Director: Jess Wolstenholm, M. Ed.
Creative Director: Jeremy Seymour
Art Director/Designer: John Trent
Illustrations: Herald Entertainment

Bible facts, historical context, and theology reviewed by Docent Research Group.

Library of Congress Cataloging-in-Publication Data has been applied for.

10 9 8 7 6 5 4 3 2
ISBN: 978-1-9626-6113-3 (Hardcover)
Printed in the USA

TABLE OF CONTENTS

WHAT IS LENT?

Lent is a special time to get our hearts ready for Easter—like when you get your playroom or backyard ready before a friend comes over. The season of Lent lasts for 40 days (not counting Sundays!) and helps us remember how much Jesus loves us. Lent starts on a day called Ash Wednesday and ends right before Easter Sunday. During Lent, we can spend time with God, pray, help others, and try to be extra kind, just like Jesus!

A long time ago, Jesus gave up His life for us, and that's what Easter is all about. So during Lent, some people give up something they really like . . . candy, screen time, or a favorite toy. It's their way of saying, "Jesus, I remember what **YOU** gave up for me!" Other people try to add something good . . . reading the Bible, helping a friend, or doing a special devotion like this one. It's their way of saying, "Jesus, thank You for loving me. I want to grow my friendship with You!"

So, whether you take something away or add something new, Lent helps us think about Jesus—every day, for 40 days—as we learn to love Him more and more. This devotional goes through Jesus' life, and will get our hearts ready to celebrate the best part of His story—Easter!

ASH WEDNESDAY is the very first day of Lent. On Ash Wednesday, some people go to church and get a tiny cross made of ashes on their forehead. It's a dusty little reminder that we need Jesus.

LITURGICAL CALENDAR

The season of Lent is a part of the liturgical calendar. The liturgical calendar, also known as the Church calendar, is a way of keeping track of the year by knowing the church holidays. It helps us to mark the seasons with Scripture and stories, giving us reminders about what to pay special attention to as we worship during particular times of the year. The seasons of the Church calendar include: **ADVENT**, **CHRISTMASTIDE**, **ORDINARY TIME**, **LENT**, **EASTERTIDE**, **PENTECOST**, and more **ORDINARY TIME**.

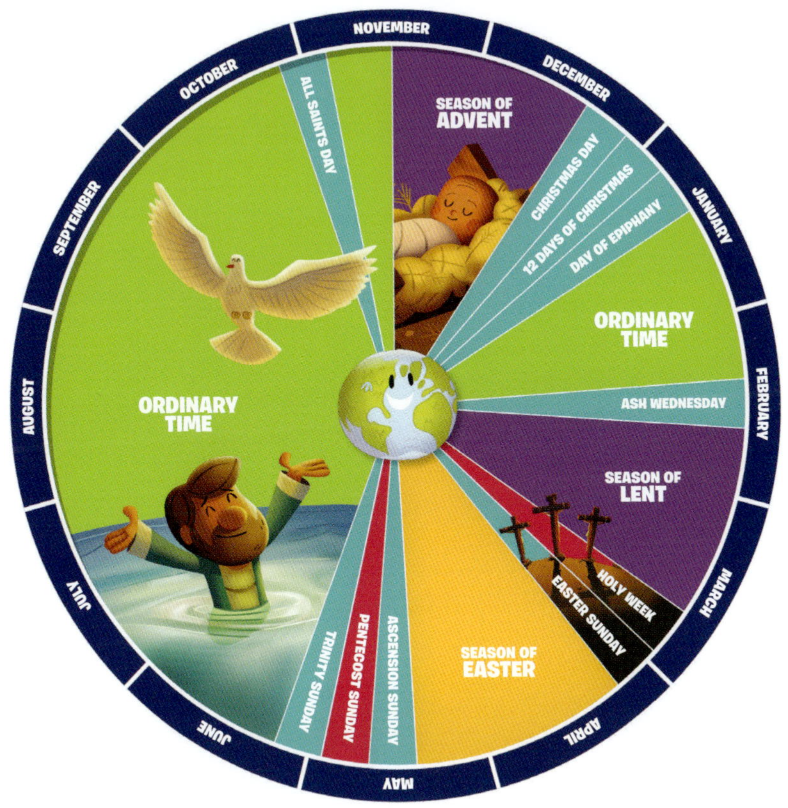

Visit **gominno.com/easter** to download a copy of the Laugh and Grow Bible Liturgical Calendar so you can follow along with the seasons this year.

WEEK 1
JOHN BAPTIZES JESUS

Before we talk about Jesus' life, let's look at another special baby who was born around the same time, named John. Some people called him John the Baptist. *Why did they call him that?* Oh, you'll see!

John was kind of a wild guy—he wore itchy clothes made from camel hair, lived out in the desert, and ate bugs and honey for lunch! Crunchy! But John was special because God gave him an important job. John helped people get their hearts ready for Jesus, just like we are doing for **EASTER** right now!

John told everyone, "Stop doing wrong things and turn back to God!" When people wanted to follow God, John baptized them. That means he dunked them in water to show they wanted a clean heart and a fresh start with God.

One day, Jesus came to John and said, "**BAPTIZE ME**." John was so surprised! "Me? Baptize You?" And Jesus said, "Yes. It's the right thing to do."

So, John baptized Jesus in the river. *And guess what?* When Jesus came out of the water, the sky opened up! God's Spirit came down like a dove, and a voice said, "This is My Son. I love Him very much!"

Wow! That was God's voice! God was letting everyone know that Jesus really is His Son and that He was ready to start His big rescue plan.

MATTHEW 3

PART 1
STAND OUT FOR JESUS

PART 2
WHAT IS BAPTISM?

This is my Son and I love him.
I am very pleased with him.
Matthew 3:17 ICB

STAND OUT FOR JESUS

Have you ever felt a little different *from everyone else?* It can be hard when we feel like we stand out. But being different can be good, especially when we're standing out for Jesus!

John the Baptist sure stood out. He didn't wear fancy clothes or live in a big city. He wore scratchy camel hair and lived out in the wilderness. He even ate bugs! People thought he was a little strange.

But John didn't mind being different. He knew God had given him a very special job—to help people get ready for Jesus. John told everyone to stop turning away from God and doing wrong things. He even baptized people in the river to show they wanted to live a **NEW LIFE** with God.

John didn't look or act like everyone else, but he was exactly who God wanted him to be. And when Jesus came, John helped people see that Jesus was the One they had been waiting for!

We can stand out for Jesus too! We can be kind when others are mean, share when others don't, or talk about Jesus even if no one else does.

It's okay to be different, especially when we stand out for Jesus!

FAMILY CONNECTION
STAND OUT FOR JESUS

TALK

1. What made John the Baptist stand out from everyone else?
2. What is one way you can stand out for Jesus this week?

SAY

I can stand out for Jesus!

PRAY

Dear God, sometimes it can be hard to feel different. Help us remember that following Jesus means standing out for good! May all we say and do point people to You! Amen.

REMEMBER

Don't live the way the world lives. Let your way of thinking be completely changed. Then you will be able to test what God wants for you.

ROMANS 12:2A NIRV

PLAY

SPOT THE DIFFERENCE

Look! It's John the Baptist times 6! Can you spot the differences and find two that are the same?

Answer: C & D

WHAT IS BAPTISM?

Have you ever seen someone get *baptized?* Maybe they went into a big pool or river, and someone dunked them underwater and brought them back up. Maybe they had water sprinkled on their head. That's called baptism! *But what does it mean?*

Remember John the Baptist? He was a different kind of guy . . . he wore clothes made of scratchy camel hair and ate bugs! But God gave John a very important job. John helped people get ready for Jesus by telling them to turn away from their sins and follow God. When people wanted a fresh start, John baptized them in the river.

BAPTISM is a special way to show that we want to follow God. When someone is dunked in the water, it's like washing away their old life and starting a new one with Jesus. It's also a way to tell others, "I belong to God's family!"

Even Jesus was baptized. That's one way we know it's really important! Baptism is a big step in showing your love for Jesus. It tells the world, "I want to follow God with my whole heart!"

FAMILY CONNECTION

WHAT IS BAPTISM?

TALK

1. Why do you think Jesus asked John to baptize Him?
2. Why is it important for Jesus followers to be baptized today?

SAY

Baptism shows the world that I follow Jesus!

PRAY

Dear God, we know that being baptized means we have a new life with Jesus! Thank You for sending Jesus to be our Savior and our friend. Amen.

REMEMBER

All of you who have been united with Christ in baptism have put on Christ, like putting on new clothes.

GALATIANS 3:27 NLT

PLAY

FINGER MAZE

Help Jesus get to the river to be baptized by John.

WEEK 2
THE DESERT TEMPTATION

What's the biggest job you've ever *tried to do?* Sometimes big jobs can be overwhelming! Jesus had the biggest job of all time . . . to save the whole world! He knew it would be hard. *So, what do you think He did first? Collect a team of superheroes? Plan a meeting with the king?* Nope. He went to the wilderness.

The wilderness was probably a lonely place, full of rocks, sand, and not much else. Just Jesus, wild animals, a whole lot of dirt, and the wind. But Jesus had a good reason for going there. God's Spirit led Him into the desert so He could prepare for everything that was about to happen.

While Jesus was in the wilderness, He didn't eat . . . at all. Not because He forgot to pack a snack, but on purpose! He wanted to spend all His time and energy praying. This is called "fasting." **FASTING** means giving up food or drinks for a specific period of time. For Jesus followers, it's a way to grow closer to God by depending on Him instead of food.

Jesus knew He'd need to be very close to His Father for this big job, so He got ready by fasting and praying in the wilderness for 40 days—hey, that's the same number of days as Lent!

While He was weak and hungry, the sneaky snake, Satan, tried to trick Jesus into using His power to make His big job easier.

But Jesus was closer to God and stronger than ever so he didn't fall for the sneaky snake's tricks! Instead, He walked away from the snake, out of the desert, ready to save the world.

MATTHEW 4:1-11

PART 1
TIME WITH GOD

PART 2
SPEAK THE TRUTH

People do not live by bread alone, but by every word that comes from the mouth of God.
Matthew 4:4 NLT

TIME WITH GOD

Do you know what's important to *your parents? What do they really care about? God? Your family? A certain sport?* You probably know what matters to your parents because you spend time with them!

When Jesus spent 40 whole days in the wilderness with His Father, God, He didn't play games, catch frogs, or sit around suntanning. Instead, He **PRAYED**. Jesus wanted to be close to God and know His heart. So when the sneaky snake came to tempt Him, Jesus was ready.

First, the sneaky snake said, "Turn these stones into bread." Jesus was super hungry! But He knew God would provide everything He needed, even without bread.

Then the sneaky snake said, "Jump off the temple! Angels will catch you!" Jesus didn't need to test God's power. He trusted it.

Finally, that sneaky snake promised Jesus all the kingdoms of the world if Jesus would bow down and worship him. But Jesus knew God's plan was **BETTER**.

Jesus knew what was important to His Father because He had spent time with Him. When you spend time with God through prayer, worship, or reading the Bible, you learn what matters most to Him too.

FAMILY CONNECTION

TIME WITH GOD

TALK

1. Why did Jesus want to spend time with His father, God?
2. What happens when we spend time with God through prayer, Bible study, and worship?

SAY

Spending time with God helps me know Him better.

PRAY

Dear God, it is a joy to get to spend time with You. May we remember that time with You helps us understand Your plan for our lives and Your love for everyone. Amen.

REMEMBER

Come close to God, and God will come close to you.

JAMES 4:8A NLT

PLAY

10, 15, 30

Name all the things you are thankful for in 10 seconds.

Say a 15-second prayer for someone you love.

Now close your eyes and pray to God for 30 seconds.

SPEAK THE TRUTH

Do you know what it means to be *tempted?* **TEMPTATION** is the desire to do something, usually something wrong. *Have you ever been tempted to do something wrong? When you are tempted, what should you do?*

Jesus has given us an example of what to do when we are tempted to do something we know is wrong.

The first thing Jesus taught us to do is to **PRAY**. Jesus prayed in the desert for 40 days, but we don't need to pray that long to get help from God. He's always ready to help us when we ask Him.

The next thing Jesus showed us how to do is to use the truth of **GOD'S WORD** to fight temptation. When that sneaky snake said, "Turn these stones into bread," Jesus quoted Scripture saying, "People do not live by bread alone." (Deuteronomy 8:3)

When the sneaky snake said, "Jump off the temple and the angels will save you!" Jesus said, "You must not test the Lord your God." (Deuteronomy 6:16)

And when the snake promised Jesus the kingdoms of the world if Jesus would worship him, Jesus said, "You must worship the Lord your God and serve only him." (Deuteronomy 6:13)

Jesus knew the Word of God and used that **TRUTH** to make the tempter go away. When we pray and speak the truth of God's Word, we can fight temptation too!

FAMILY CONNECTION
SPEAK THE TRUTH

TALK

1. What does it mean to be tempted?
2. How did Jesus respond to the sneaky snake's temptation?

SAY

When I pray and speak God's Word, I can fight temptation.

PRAY

Dear God, thank You that we can talk to You in prayer and read the Bible to help us when we are in tough situations. May we always choose what's right according to Your Word. Amen.

REMEMBER

I have stored up your word in my heart, that I might not sin against you.

PSALM 119:11 ESV

PLAY

3, 2, 1...

Name **3** ways the sneaky snake tried to trick Jesus.

What **2** things did Jesus do to fight temptation?

Shout **1** thing to the sneaky snake to tell him to go away.

WEEK 3
JESUS' DISCIPLES

After Jesus walked out of the wilderness, He traveled through Israel, saying, "The Kingdom of God is here!" That made people curious.

Soon, people began following Him. Some had big questions about God's kingdom. Others followed because Jesus healed the sick. And some followed just because Jesus looked at them and said, "Follow Me."

One day, Jesus walked past some fishermen. He called, "Follow Me!" Simon Peter, Andrew, James, and John dropped their nets so fast there were probably floppy fish still inside!

Then Jesus saw Matthew at his tax booth. "Follow Me!" Matthew stood up, left his coins behind, and never looked back. Jesus also invited Philip (who brought Bartholomew), Thomas, Thaddeus, Judas, another James, and another Simon. These 12 were His closest followers, called "disciples." A **DISCIPLE** is someone who follows Jesus.

And what did they do? Play follow-the-leader all day? Not exactly, though they did walk a lot. They ate together, healed people, and told others about God's kingdom. The disciples learned to live and love like Jesus.

Did you know Jesus says "Follow Me" to you too? You may not see Him in person, but you can still be His disciple. When you read the Bible and talk to Him in prayer, you'll learn to live and love like Jesus too!

LUKE 5:1-11

PART 1
ORDINARY PEOPLE

PART 2
A LEADER LIKE NO OTHER

Follow me, and I will make you fishers of men.
Matthew 4:19 ESV

ORDINARY PEOPLE

If you were going to choose people *for a team to help you save the world, who would you choose first? A superhero, an important leader, or a super-smart scientist?* Those choices would make sense. But that isn't what Jesus did when He set out to save the world.

Instead of choosing really powerful people, Jesus started with ordinary fishermen. *Do you think these fishermen were trained to save the world?* Nope. They were probably really good at fixing nets and catching fish. Maybe not so good at rescuing people. But the way Jesus does things doesn't usually look like the way we would do them. Jesus didn't need people who were famous or good at lots of stuff. He needed people who would listen to Him and be willing to learn. Just **ORDINARY** people.

So, Jesus chose a few fishermen and said, "Come follow Me." Then Jesus asked a tax collector to be on His team. Nobody liked tax collectors because they often cheated people out of their money, but Jesus chose Matthew. *Do you think Matthew was trained to save the world?* Nope. But Jesus picked Matthew because He knew Matthew would follow Him.

God likes to pick ordinary people for extraordinary jobs. He doesn't look at our abilities or strengths. He looks at our heart. You're an ordinary person, just like the fishermen—Peter, Andrew, James, and John—or the tax collector, Matthew. God wants you to be on His team too! *Will you follow Him?*

FAMILY CONNECTION
ORDINARY PEOPLE

TALK

1. Why do you think Jesus picked ordinary people to be His disciples?
2. What is one thing you can do this week to learn more about the way of Jesus?

SAY

I am a disciple of Jesus, learning to follow His way every day!

PRAY

Dear God, thank You for choosing ordinary people like us to be Your disciples. We want to follow You so we can learn to live Your way! Amen.

REMEMBER

I am the light of the world. Whoever follows me will not walk in darkness, but will have the light of life.

JOHN 8:12 ESV

PLAY
FOLLOW THE LINE

Which path leads Jesus to each of His disciples?

Answer: A|Matthew, B|James, C|Peter

A LEADER LIKE NO OTHER

Have you ever played a game *where someone was the leader? How did they act? Were they kind, mean, or bossy?* Some leaders like to be in charge and tell everyone what to do. Some leaders are unfair! But not Jesus! Jesus was a different kind of leader.

Before Jesus chose His twelve disciples, He spent a whole day praying, asking God to help Him pick. Jesus was a leader who was **CLOSE** to God.

People in Jesus' time usually thought that only men should be allowed to follow an important leader like Jesus. But when women and children started to follow Jesus, He said, "Let them come!" Jesus was a leader who didn't feel "too important" to bless children or talk with women.

Sometimes the disciples scratched their heads, confused about what Jesus was saying or doing. But He didn't get frustrated with them. Jesus was always **SERVING** His disciples. One time He washed their stinky feet—including Peter's feet—even though Jesus knew Peter was about to tell people they weren't friends. Jesus was a leader who was very patient with His followers.

Jesus was powerful enough to calm stormy seas and bring people back to life, yet He was the kind of leader who prayed, included people who were often forgotten, and served everyone.

Now that's a leader worth following!

FAMILY CONNECTION
A LEADER LIKE NO OTHER

TALK

1. Why do you think Jesus was such a special leader?
2. What can we learn from Jesus about how to treat others?

SAY

Jesus is the best leader, so I will follow Him!

PRAY

Dear God, thank You for sending Your Son, Jesus, to be the best leader and example for us. Please help us follow Jesus faithfully every day so we can be leaders like Him. Amen.

REMEMBER

Live a life filled with love, following the example of Christ.

EPHESIANS 5:2A NLT

PLAY
SOUND OR STORY

Close your eyes and point to one of the pictures below. Then make up a sound or tell a story using that object or person.

WEEK 4
SERMON ON THE MOUNT

One day when Jesus was teaching His followers, He climbed up a big hill so the huge crowd could hear Him. Jesus sat down and gave them a very special message. Today, we call it the "Sermon on the Mount." It's full of important truths about what it means to live in God's kingdom.

Jesus said lots of surprising things in His Sermon on the Mount. "If you're feeling left out or sad, guess what? You're blessed! God's kingdom is for **YOU!**"

He talked about people who don't push to be first and people who are kind and gentle. Jesus said that, in *His* kingdom, the people who seem the least important are actually the most special! Whoa!

Then Jesus said even more amazing things. "Love your enemies. Share your stuff. Be kind, even when others aren't." It was as if Jesus was talking about an upside-down world, where the last become first and the sad become glad.

Jesus wasn't just giving people rules to follow. He was giving them instructions on how to have *new hearts*! That means loving like Jesus, forgiving like Jesus, and putting others first, just like Jesus!

Jesus wants you to know that in God's kingdom, **YOU** are super-duper important. And Jesus wants to help you live like you know it . . . so you can love others like He does.

MATTHEW 5-7

PART 1
UPSIDE DOWN KINGDOM

PART 2
RELATIONSHIP OVER RULES

Do to others whatever you would like them to do to you.
Matthew 7:12A NLT

UPSIDE DOWN KINGDOM

Have you ever stood on your head *or hung upside down on the monkey bars?* Everything looks funny and different and it kinda makes your head spin! Well, God's kingdom is like that—upside down! But God's upside-down kingdom won't make your head hurt.

In our world, people think being the biggest, fastest, or loudest is what matters. But in **GOD'S KINGDOM**, the quiet, gentle, and kind people are the most special. Jesus said, "If you're last in line now, you'll be first in God's kingdom!" That sounds backwards, but it's true!

Jesus also said to love people who aren't nice, to share even when it's hard, and to forgive others just like God forgives us. That's not always easy, but it's how Jesus lived—and He wants us to live that way too.

God's **UPSIDE-DOWN** kingdom means we don't have to be the best to be loved. We just need to have hearts that love like Jesus. In His kingdom, being kind is stronger than being tough. And being gentle is better than being bossy.

So if you ever feel small, quiet, or left out—remember, in God's kingdom, **YOU** are important. Because in His upside-down kingdom, you are known and loved by Him!

FAMILY CONNECTION

UPSIDE DOWN KINGDOM

TALK

1. What are some ways God's kingdom is different from the world?
2. What "upside-down" thing can you do this week to love someone like Jesus?

SAY

God's upside-down kingdom puts love first!

PRAY

Dear God, we are so thankful that Your kingdom is different from everything around us. Help us to remember what it means to live in Your upside-down world. Amen.

REMEMBER

But seek first the kingdom of God and his righteousness, and all these things will be added to you.

MATTHEW 6:33 ESV

PLAY

WHAT AM I LOOKING AT?

Look at each of the upside-down pictures below and say what you see.

RELATIONSHIP OVER RULES

Have you ever played a game *with lots of rules?* Rules can help us know what to do, but following rules isn't always the most important thing, especially when it comes to knowing Jesus!

A long time ago, people thought that to be close to God, they had to follow all the rules perfectly. But then Jesus came and showed them something better. Jesus didn't come to bring more rules. Jesus came to make a way for us to have a **RELATIONSHIP** with God and to give us a new heart.

Jesus wants to be your friend, not just your rule-keeper. That means He wants to spend time with you, talk to you, help you when you're sad, and celebrate when you're happy. He wants to be close to you—not because you're perfect, but because He loves you.

When you know Jesus and love Him, you'll want to do the right things—not just to follow the rules, but to make His heart happy! Loving Jesus helps us become more like Him—kind, gentle, forgiving, and full of joy.

Being good is great, but knowing Jesus is even better! He's not looking for perfect rule-followers—He's looking for forever friends. And that includes **YOU!**

FAMILY CONNECTION
RELATIONSHIP OVER RULES

TALK

1. Why do you think our relationship with Jesus is more important than following rules?
2. What does it look like to be Jesus' friend?

SAY

My friendship with Jesus helps me live God's way!

PRAY

Dear God, thank You for providing a way for us to be friends with Jesus and with You. We want to live Your way, not just by following the rules, but by being a friend of Jesus every day. Amen.

REMEMBER

Yes, I am the vine; you are the branches. Those who remain in me, and I in them, will produce much fruit. For apart from me you can do nothing.

JOHN 15:5 NLT

PLAY

FINGER MAZE

Help the people get to Jesus teaching on the hill.

WEEK 5
IT'S A MIRACLE!

Did you know Jesus did AMAZING *things?* Big, wow-worthy, super-duper things called miracles! **MIRACLE** is a fancy word for something only God can do—something that shows just how powerful He is.

One day, Jesus and His friends were on a boat when a HUGE storm showed up! The waves were big, the wind was loud, and the disciples were scared. *But what was Jesus doing?* **SLEEPING!**

Sleeping! When the disciples woke Him up, Jesus stood and said, "Stop!" And the storm listened! Whoosh! Everything got quiet. Jesus showed He is King over storms!

Another time, thousands of people were hungry. A boy gave Jesus his lunch—just five little loaves of bread and two tiny fish. Jesus prayed, and then—wow!—there was enough food for **EVERYONE**. Another miracle! Jesus showed He is the King of giving and caring for our needs.

And once, a man's little girl had died. But Jesus took her hand and brought her back to life! Just like that! Jesus showed He is King over sickness and even death.

Some people didn't like what Jesus was doing. But that didn't stop Him! Jesus came to show us what God's kingdom is like—full of love, full of life . . . full of miracles!

When you are scared or in need, don't forget: Jesus is the King of everything, and He's always with you!

MARK 4-6

PART 1
KING OF EVERYTHING

PART 2
WHEN MIRACLES DON'T HAPPEN

What is impossible with man is possible with God.
Luke 18:27 ESV

KING OF EVERYTHING

Have you ever seen a king in a *storybook or movie?* Kings wear shiny crowns, live in castles, and give big commands. *But did you know we have a real, forever King?* His name is Jesus!

Jesus isn't just any king. He's the **KING** of everything! He's the King over the sky and the sea, the sun and the stars, the birds and the bugs—even the storms listen to Him!

When Jesus was on earth, He showed us what God's kingdom is like. He calmed wild waves, made sick people better, gave food to thousands, and even brought people back to life. **WOW!** No one else can do that—only King Jesus!

But here's the best part: Jesus isn't just powerful, He's loving too. He's a King who cares about **YOU**. He hears your prayers, knows your heart, and wants to be your forever friend.

Some kings sit on big fancy thrones, but Jesus came to serve and love others. That's what makes Him the best King of all.

FAMILY CONNECTION
KING OF EVERYTHING

TALK

1. How did Jesus' miracles show us what God's kingdom is like?
2. How does it make you feel to know that Jesus, the King of everything, knows and loves YOU?

SAY

Jesus is the King of everything!

PRAY

Dear God, thank You that Jesus is the King of everything, and we can trust Him to do amazing things! Amen.

REMEMBER

Jesus came and told his disciples, "I have been given all authority in heaven and on earth."

MATTHEW 28:18 NLT

PLAY

SPOT THE DIFFERENCE

Can you spot the differences and find two crowns that are the same?

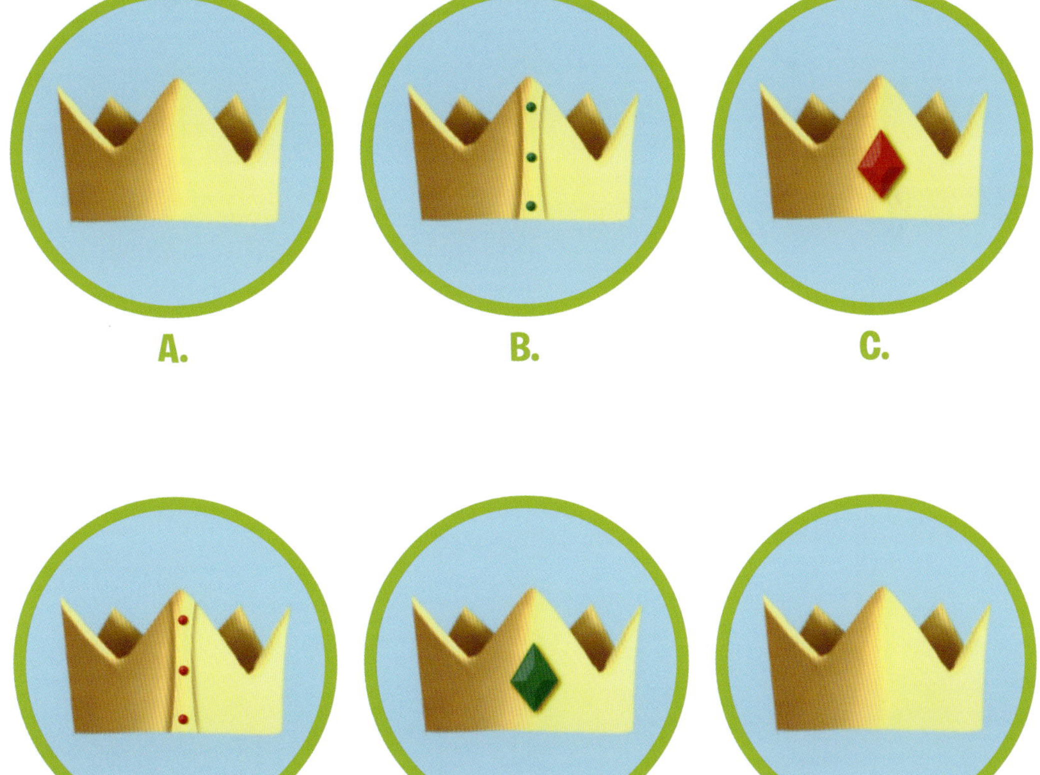

Answer: A & F

WHEN MIRACLES DON'T HAPPEN

Have you ever prayed for *something big—a sick loved one to be healed, or maybe that your family would finally get a puppy?* We can ask God anything . . . to help someone feel better, stop a storm, or make a problem go away. And sometimes, God says yes! But other times . . . His answer doesn't look like what we'd hoped.

That can feel sad or confusing. You might wonder, "Did God hear me? Did I do something wrong?" But here's the truth: God **ALWAYS** hears your prayers. He always loves you. And He is always with you—even when His answer is "no" or "not yet."

God sees the whole picture when we can only see a little bit. He knows what's best, even when we don't understand. And sometimes, God uses hard things to help us grow stronger or to show us His love in a different way.

When miracles don't happen, we can still trust that God is good. We can keep praying, keep hoping, and keep remembering that God's love never stops.

If your heart feels sad, talk to Jesus. He understands. And He will hold you close, no matter what.

FAMILY CONNECTION

WHEN MIRACLES DON'T HAPPEN

TALK

1. Share about a time you asked God for something and His answer wasn't what you'd hoped for.
2. Why do you think we can still trust God even when He doesn't do what we ask Him to do?

SAY

I can trust God because He is good, no matter what!

PRAY

Dear God, we know that sometimes You don't answer our prayers the way we'd like You to because You see more than we can see. Please help us to trust You, no matter what! Amen.

REMEMBER

Trust the Lord with all your heart; do not depend on your own understanding.

PROVERBS 3:5 NLT

PLAY

FOLLOW THE LINE

Which path leads Jesus to each of the miracles?

Answer: A|Heal the Girl, B|Calm the Storm, C|Feed 5000

WEEK 6
HOLY WEEK

Have you ever had a week that *completely changed your life?* Maybe a new baby joined your family, you moved to a new house, or you learned how to read.

Jesus had a week that changed the entire world. It all started the day He rode into Jerusalem on a donkey. During the next few days, He flipped over tables in the temple, washed His disciples' stinky-smelly feet, shared bread, prayed so hard He sweated out blood, got arrested, and died.

Through it all, Jesus showed His **AMAZING** power and love for those around Him. But the best part of that whole week was at the end of it . . . when He came back to life!

The week that changed everything was wild for the disciples too. One day, people were waving palm branches and cheering for their friend Jesus. A few days later, they were shouting for Him to die. Jesus' friends felt confused, scared, and sad. But Jesus wasn't surprised.

None of the big, bad, awful things, like getting arrested or dying, surprised Jesus. In fact, getting arrested and dying was actually God's good plan from the start. As God's Son, Jesus knew this wild week was going to happen. He also knew why it had to happen. Because God loved the world so much, He gave His only **SON**. Everyone who believes that Jesus died and came back to life gets to be part of the new Kingdom that God promised! God's kingdom is where Jesus is King and everything is made right.

MATTHEW 21-28

PALM SUNDAY

HOLY MONDAY

HOLY TUESDAY

HOLY WEDNESDAY

MAUNDY THURSDAY

GOOD FRIDAY

HOLY SATURDAY

For God loved the world so much that he gave his only Son. God gave his Son so that whoever believes in him may not be lost, but have eternal life.
John 3:16 ICB

PALM SUNDAY

One day, Jesus asked His disciples to untie a stranger's donkey, and they did it, just like that. Of course, the owner said, "Excuse me! Why are you untying my donkey?" The disciples answered, "The Lord needs it," just as Jesus had told them to say. And that was enough. Jesus was so famous that people even let Him borrow their animals.

Have you ever met someone famous? What did you do? Did you shout or scream? When Jesus came into Jerusalem on that donkey, the people went wild. Jesus was like a celebrity! He had done amazing miracles and even raised his buddy Lazarus from the dead. And He was coming into their city. **WOW!**

Some people threw coats on the road for the donkey to walk on. Others cut palm branches off trees and waved them in the air. They shouted, "**HOSANNA!**" which was a way of praising and celebrating Him, kind of like we do in church. They treated Jesus like a hero who had won a great battle. Even after the grown-ups stopped cheering, kids kept shouting, "Hosanna to the Son of David!" They followed Jesus all the way to the temple.

The people were so excited to see Jesus, and they didn't even know the whole story yet. They had seen Jesus do amazing miracles, but soon, they'd see that Jesus had even more power than that!

FAMILY CONNECTION
PALM SUNDAY

TALK

1. Why do you think the people shouted and waved palm branches when they saw Jesus entering the city?
2. What do you think you would do if you were able to see Jesus in person?

SAY

Jesus deserves our celebration!

PRAY

Dear God, we want always to welcome Jesus into our lives with great celebration. May we remember that He deserves our praise every day! Amen.

REMEMBER

So they took branches of palm trees and went out to meet him, crying out, "Hosanna! Blessed is he who comes in the name of the Lord . . ."

JOHN 12:13 ESV

PLAY
SOUND OR STORY

Close your eyes and point to one of the pictures below. Then make up a sound or tell a story using that object or person.

HOLY MONDAY

Have you ever gone on a scavenger *hunt where you are given a list of items to find?* Scavenger hunts can be a lot of fun! One day, Jesus sent two of His disciples on a scavenger hunt.

Jesus had come to Jerusalem to celebrate **PASSOVER**—a special Jewish holiday remembering how God freed the Israelites from slavery in Egypt. It was time for the Passover meal. But in Jesus' time, there were no restaurants. People always had to make meals themselves! *Since none of the disciples lived in Jerusalem, where would they prepare dinner*?

Jesus had a plan, but He needed His disciples to trust Him. He gave them some funny instructions:

Go into the city. A man carrying a jar of water will meet you. Follow him. When he goes into a house, talk to the person who owns the house. That's where you're going to set up our special Passover meal!

See? It was like a scavenger hunt! By now, the disciples were used to Jesus' unusual instructions, so they obeyed. Everything happened just like He said. When they got to the house, the room was already ready—they just needed to make the meal.

Sometimes, Jesus' instructions don't make sense to us. But when we **TRUST** Him, we'll see how God works everything together for the good of those who love Him.

FAMILY CONNECTION
HOLY MONDAY

TALK

1. Why do you think Jesus gave His disciples these instructions to prepare for the Passover meal?
2. What is something you've had to trust God for?

SAY

God's instructions lead me in the best way!

PRAY

Dear God, sometimes we don't understand what You are asking us to do. Please help us remember that we can trust You because You will always lead us in the best way! Amen.

REMEMBER

And we know that God causes everything to work together for the good of those who love God and are called according to his purpose for them.

ROMANS 8:28 NLT

PLAY

WHAT DID JESUS SAY?

Read each phrase and decide if Jesus said it or not.

- **Come follow Me.**
- **I will make you fishers of men.**
- **Would you like a peanut butter and jelly sandwich?**
- **Love one another.**
- **I am the light of the world.**
- **Eat your vegetables.**
- **Did you clean your room?**
- **Wanna see Me hula hoop?**

HOLY TUESDAY

During their Passover celebration meal, Jesus did something surprising for His disciples. In the middle of dinner He got on His knees and washed their feet!

Washing feet? Yuck! Feet are stinky and dirty, especially because the disciples were walking around outside all day in sandals. Usually, only a servant would do that job. But Jesus, the **SON OF GOD**, the King of everything, bent down low and washed His friends' feet.

Why? Because Jesus wanted to show them what **LOVE** looks like. He wanted them to know that in God's kingdom, being great means serving others, not being the boss of everyone. Jesus was teaching them to be kind, humble, and full of love, just like He is.

Jesus said, "I'm your teacher, and I washed your feet. Now you should wash one another's feet." That doesn't mean we always have to wash real feet—but it does mean we should help people, be kind, and think of others first.

Jesus showed us what love looks like all through Holy Week—and on Easter, we celebrate the greatest love of all because Jesus died for us and rose again to give us new life!

FAMILY CONNECTION
HOLY TUESDAY

TALK

1. Why did Jesus wash His disciples' feet?
2. What is one way you can love or serve someone this week?

SAY

Jesus shows me what it means to love and serve others.

PRAY

Dear God, we are so thankful that Jesus came to show us what humble love looks like. Please teach us what it means to love and serve others like Jesus. Amen.

REMEMBER

For even the Son of Man came not to be served but to serve others and to give his life as a ransom for many.

MATTHEW 20:28 NLT

PLAY

FOLLOW THE LINE

Which path leads to the foot washing bowl? The towel? The soap?

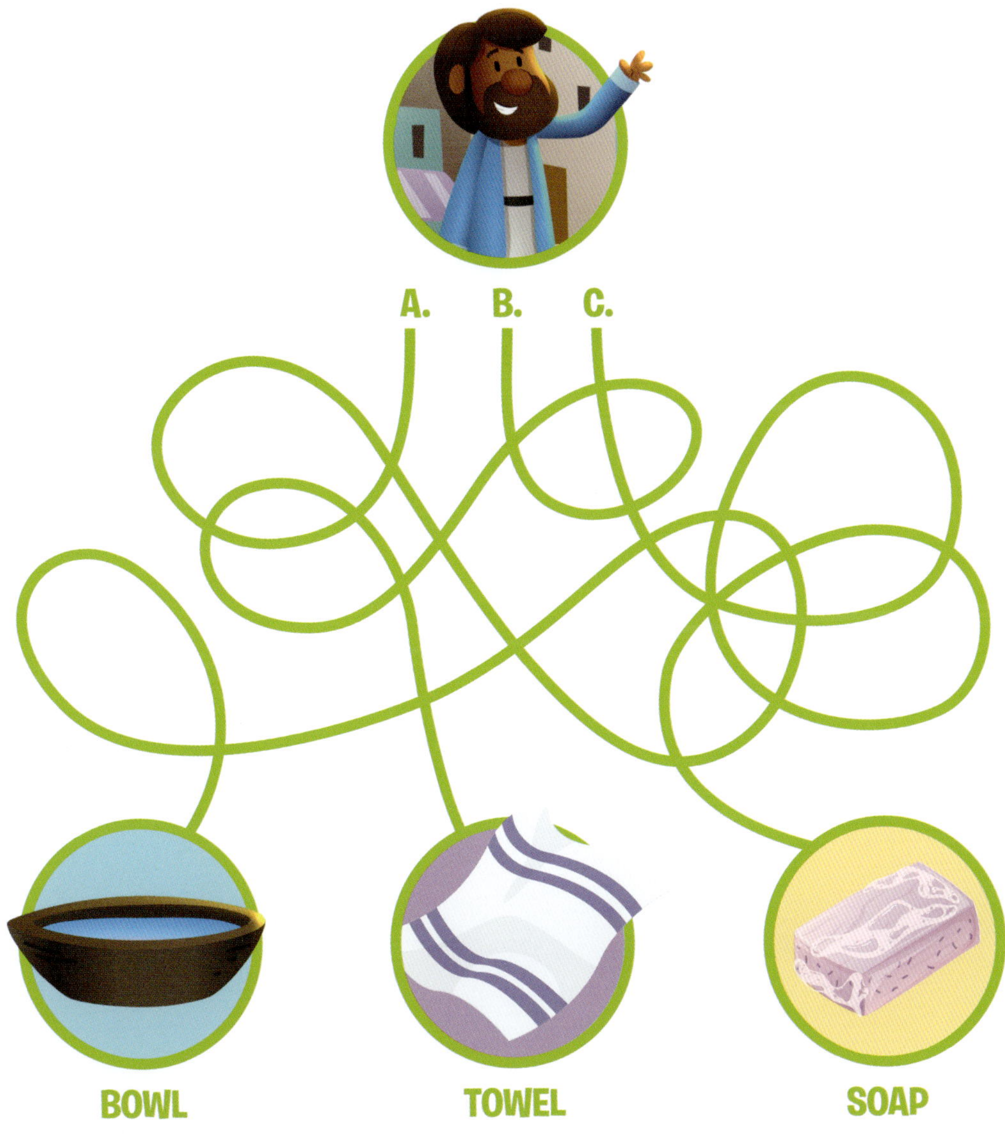

Answer: A|Bowl, B|Towel, C|Soap

HOLY WEDNESDAY

The special dinner Jesus had with His disciples for Passover is now called, The Last Supper. During this very special time, Jesus not only washed His disciples' feet, He also shared some very special things with His friends because something big was about to happen.

During the meal, Jesus picked up some bread. He broke it and said, "This is My body, given for you." Then He took a cup of wine and said, "This is My blood, poured out for you." He told His disciples to eat and drink to **REMEMBER** Him.

Wait—bread and wine? What do those have to do with Jesus? How would they help the disciples remember Him? Jesus was giving His friends a way to remember what was about to happen. He was going to give His body and blood on the cross—for us! He was showing the disciples how much He loved them and that He would always be with them.

Today, we call this **COMMUNION**, the Lord's Supper, or the Eucharist. When we take communion at church—eating the bread and drinking from the cup—we remember what Jesus did on the cross and we celebrate the new life we have because of Him!

FAMILY CONNECTION
HOLY WEDNESDAY

TALK

1. What does the bread remind us of? What does the wine remind us of?
2. Why do you think it's important to take communion?

SAY

I will remember what Jesus did for me on the cross!

PRAY

Dear God, thank You that Jesus gave His life for us on the cross. Help us to remember, through communion and every day, how You love us so much that You sent Your Son to take our place. Amen.

REMEMBER

But God showed his love for us by sending Christ to die for us while we were still sinners.

ROMANS 5:8 NLT

PLAY

3, 2, 1...

Name 3 foods you'd like to eat if you were having dinner with Jesus.

What 2 things do we eat and drink during communion?

Say 1 way you know Jesus loves you.

MAUNDY THURSDAY

What do you do when you're sad *or scared? Hug your mom? Say a prayer? Hide under your bed?* After the special Passover meal, Jesus was sad. He knew the next day would be really hard. He knew He was going to die.

Jesus took His friends to a garden and asked them to keep watch. Then He walked away to **TALK** to His Father, God. He was so sad and scared that He fell to the ground. *Have you ever felt that way?*

In that hard moment, Jesus did the best thing—He prayed. He even asked God if there was another way to save the world. Then He said, "Do what You want, not what I want."

When Jesus returned, were His friends praying? Nope. *Talking about dinner?* Nope. They were . . . sleeping. Jesus woke them and asked them to pray, then went off again.

He came back. They were still sleeping. *The third time?* Still sleeping! (Like they thought it was a pajama party!)

But Jesus didn't get mad. He knew He needed strength for what was coming—and **PRAYER** was the way to get it. The disciples forgot that. They were too tired to bring their worries to God.

The best thing to do when we're sad or scared is to pray. Remember—you can talk to God anytime, anywhere . . . even if you're sleepy!

FAMILY CONNECTION
MAUNDY THURSDAY

TALK

1. Why do you think Jesus spent so much time talking to God in the garden?
2. What can you remember the next time you feel sad or scared?

SAY

Talking to God helps me when I'm sad or scared!

PRAY

Dear God, thank You that we can talk to You anytime, anywhere! The next time we feel sad or scared, help us remember to bring our feelings to You. Amen.

REMEMBER

Give all your worries and cares to God because He cares for you.

1 PETER 5:7 NLT

PLAY
SOUND OR STORY

Close your eyes and point to one of the pictures below. Then make up a sound or tell a story using that object or person.

GOOD FRIDAY

super-sad day that later turned out to be good?

The day Jesus died was really awful. He was arrested and taken to a governor named Pilate, who decided to crucify Him just to keep the religious leaders happy. Then Jesus was taken up a hill to die on a wooden cross.

What a super-awful, super-sad day! Most of Jesus' disciples ran away. They didn't understand. Jesus had said He came to **SAVE** the world—*but how could He do that if He wasn't alive?*

But even on that terrible day, Jesus was doing something very good.

Our relationship with God was broken when sin entered the world. Sin is saying, "I don't care what You say—I'll do it my way!" Sin turns us away from God. Ever since Adam and Eve trusted that sneaky snake instead of God, sin has been a problem.

To save the world, Jesus had to fix that problem. When He died, Jesus took all our sins on Himself. Not because He had to—but because He wanted to. He died to take care of our sins because **HE LOVES US** so much!

That's why that super-awful, super-sad day is now called "Good Friday." It's good because Jesus paid the price for our sins. It's good because it shows how much Jesus loves us. And it's good because . . . it's not the end of the story.

FAMILY CONNECTION
GOOD FRIDAY

TALK

1. Why can we call the day Jesus died "Good Friday?"
2. How does it make you feel to know that Jesus died for you?

SAY

Good Friday is not the end of the story!

PRAY

Dear God, thinking about Jesus dying on the cross makes us so sad. Please help us remember we can call that day "good" because it wasn't the end of the story. We look forward to Easter with hope. Amen.

REMEMBER

Christ suffered for our sins once for all time. He never sinned, but he died for sinners to bring you safely home to God.

1 PETER 3:18A NLT

PLAY

SING & SHOW

Sing the song together. Come up with hand motions or actions, and try to "sing" it without the words!

Jesus loves me, this I know.
For the BIble tells me so.
Little ones to Him belong.
They are weak, but He is strong.
Yes, Jesus loves me!
Yes, Jesus loves me!
Yes, Jesus loves me!
The Bible tells me so.

HOLY SATURDAY

Saturday was a strange day.

After Jesus died on the cross, His friends were so sad. They didn't understand what was going to happen next. Friday was full of tears, and Sunday would be full of joy—*but Saturday?* Saturday was **QUIET**.

This special day is called Holy Saturday. It was the day between the sadness of the cross and the happiness of the empty tomb. A day of waiting. A day of wondering. A day of hope.

Jesus' friends didn't know yet that something amazing was about to happen. All they could do was wait and remember everything Jesus had said.

Have you ever had to wait for something? Like your birthday or a trip? Or a grade on an important test? Waiting is hard, but it helps to slow down, be still, and trust that God is working while we wait.

On Holy Saturday, we can think about how quiet the world felt without Jesus. But we also remember that God was working behind the scenes. **HOPE** was on the way!

So today, take a deep breath. Be still. Think about Jesus and all He's done for you. The story is not over yet!

FAMILY CONNECTION
HOLY SATURDAY

TALK

1. How do you think Jesus' friends felt after He died?
2. What do you need to trust God about right now?

SAY

God is still working while I wait!

PRAY

Dear God, it can be so hard to wait! Please help us to trust that You are working, even when we can't see it. Thank You for the miracle of Jesus' death and resurrection. Amen.

REMEMBER

Wait patiently for the Lord. Be brave and courageous. Yes, wait patiently for the Lord.

PSALM 27:14 NLT

PLAY 10, 15, 30

Can you be quiet for 10 seconds?

Now stare at each other and try to be quiet for 15 seconds.

Close your eyes and try to be quiet for 30 seconds.

EASTER SUNDAY: HE IS ALIVE!

Today is Easter Sunday–

the happiest day of all! *Why?* Because Jesus is **ALIVE!**

A long time ago, Jesus died on a cross. It was very sad. His friends were heartbroken. They placed His body in a tomb and rolled a big stone in front of it. Everything felt quiet. It looked like the end.

But then—surprise!—on the third day, something amazing happened. Some women came to visit the tomb, and the heavy stone had been rolled away. The tomb was empty! Jesus wasn't there!

An angel appeared to the women and said, "Don't be afraid. Jesus isn't here—He is risen!"

WOW! Jesus came back to life, just like He said He would. He showed everyone that nothing—not even death—can stop His love!

Jesus' resurrection means we can live with Him forever. It means joy wins, love wins, and Jesus wins! That's why we celebrate Easter with big smiles, happy songs, and maybe even jelly beans—because Jesus' love is sweeter than anything!

So today, let's celebrate the best news ever: Jesus is alive, and He loves **YOU!**

FAMILY CONNECTION
EASTER SUNDAY

TALK

1. Why do we celebrate Easter?
2. What is one way you can share the joy of Easter with someone this week?

SAY

Jesus is alive, and He loves ME very much!

PRAY

Dear God, thank You for sending Jesus to die on the cross for our sins and rise again to bring hope to the world. Thank You for loving us so much. Help us to share the joy of Your love with everyone! Amen.

REMEMBER

He isn't here! He is risen from the dead, just as he said would happen.

MATTHEW 28:6 NLT

PLAY

FINGER MAZE

Help Mary get back to Jesus' friends to tell them He is alive!

WHAT COMES NEXT?

Easter is such a happy day!

We celebrate that Jesus is alive! *But guess what?* The good news of Easter doesn't stop there. After the candy is gone and the eggs are put away, **EASTER** joy can keep going!

The Bible says in 1 Peter 1:3, " . . . He has given us new life and a hope that lives on!" (CEV)

That means, because Jesus came back to life, we can have a new life, too—a life full of hope! **HOPE** is knowing that, no matter what happens, something good is coming!

Even when we feel sad, scared, or unsure, we can remember: Jesus is **ALIVE!** And He is with us always!

Living with hope after Easter means you smile more, share more, forgive more, and love others just like Jesus loves you. You get to be a helper, a listener, and a bright light in the world—because Jesus' love fills your heart!

Easter isn't just one day. It's the start of something wonderful. It's a reminder that Jesus gives us hope that never ends!

FAMILY CONNECTION

WHAT COMES NEXT?

TALK

1. What does it mean to have hope?
2. Why do you think Jesus' resurrection gives us hope?

SAY

He has given me new life and a forever hope!

PRAY

Dear God, thank You that Jesus' life, death, and resurrection give us a new life and a hope that never goes away! Help us to honor You with our life by sharing Jesus' love with others every day! Amen.

REMEMBER

. . . He has given us new life and a hope that lives on.

1 PETER 1:3B CEV

PLAY
SPOT THE DIFFERENCE

This is the Hopeful World! The world we can look forward to because of Jesus . . . a world without sin and sickness and sadness. Can you spot the differences and find two that are the same?

Answer: B & D

EASTER MEMORY JOURNAL

Use this Easter journal to record your favorite verses, quotes, pictures, and other memories from your time celebrating Jesus each season.

OUR EASTER MEMORIES

Date: ____________________

OUR EASTER MEMORIES

Date: ____________________

OUR EASTER MEMORIES

Date:____________________

OUR EASTER MEMORIES

Date:__________________

OUR EASTER MEMORIES

Date:____________________